GETTING TO KNOW

SPAIN

Keith Lye

PASSPORT BOOKS
a division of *NTC Publishing Group*
Lincolnwood, Illinois USA

Editor: Lynne Williams
Design: Edward Kinsey
Illustrations: Hayward Art Group
Series Consultant: Keith Lye

Photographs: Chris Fairclough, All-Sport, The
Bettman Archive, Bridgeman Art Library,
J. Allan Cash, DAS Photo, Mary Evans, Ford,
Mary Glasgow, Popperfoto, Spanish Tourist
Office, Sonia Halliday, Rex Features, Zefa

Front cover: Chris Fairclough
Back cover: Chris Fairclough

1992 Printing

This edition first published in 1990 by Passport Books,
a division of NTC Publishing Group,
4255 West Touhy Avenue, Lincolnwood (Chicago), Illinois 60646-1975 U.S.A.
Copyright © 1990, 1987 Franklin Watts Limited.
Library of Congress Catalog Card Number: 89-61899
Manufactured in Hong Kong.

1 2 3 4 5 6 7 8 9 WKT 9 8 7 6 5 4 3 2 1

Contents

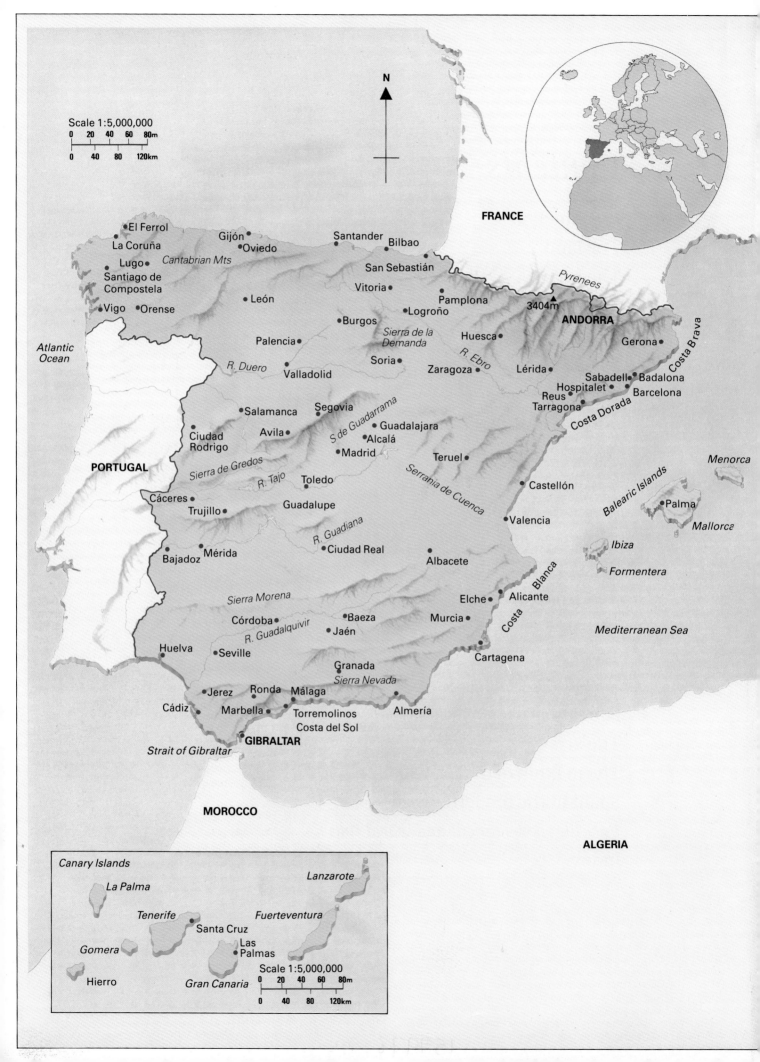

Scale 1:5,000,000

0 20 40 60 80m

0 40 80 120km

N

FRANCE

El Ferrol
La Coruña
Gijón
Oviedo
Santander Bilbao
Cantabrian Mts
San Sebastián
Lugo
Santiago de
Compostela
Vitoria
Pamplona
Logroño
Pyrenees
3404m
ANDORRA
León
Burgos
Huesca
Gerona
Costa Brava
Palencia
*Sierra de la
Demanda*
R. Ebro
Lérida
Sabadell
Badalona
Vigo
Orense
Soria
Zaragoza
Hospitalet
Barcelona
R. Duero
Valladolid
Reus
Tarragona
Costa Dorada

*Atlantic
Ocean*

Salamanca
Segovia
S de Guadarrama
Guadalajara
Ciudad
Rodrigo
Avila
Alcalá
Madrid
Teruel
Castellón
Balearic Islands
Menorca
PORTUGAL
Sierra de Gredos
R. Tajo
Toledo
Serrania de Cuenca
Palma
Cáceres
Guadalupe
Valencia
Mallorca
Trujillo
R. Guadiana
Ibiza
Bajadoz
Mérida
Ciudad Real
Albacete
Formentera
Sierra Morena
Blanca
Córdoba
Baeza
Elche
Alicante
Mediterranean Sea
R. Guadalquivir
Jaén
Murcia
Costa
Huelva
Seville
Cartagena
Jerez
Ronda
Granada
Málaga
Sierra Nevada
Cádiz
Marbella
Torremolinos
Almería
Costa del Sol
GIBRALTAR
Strait of Gibraltar

MOROCCO

ALGERIA

Canary Islands
Lanzarote
La Palma
Tenerife
Fuerteventura
Santa Cruz
Gomera
Las
Palmas
Hierro
Gran Canaria

Scale 1:5,000,000

0 20 40 60 80m

0 40 80 120km

Introduction

Spain, the second largest country in western Europe after France, occupies about 85 per cent of the Iberian peninsula – the rest belongs to Portugal. Spain also includes the Balearic and Canary Islands.

Spain is known as a land of beaches and castles, religious processions and bullfights, wine and olives. But today it is also a nation on the move. Since the late 1950s, Spain has changed from a poor farming country into an urban, industrial one.

Society has also changed, especially since the restoration of democracy in the mid-1970s, following 36 years of dictatorship. New ideas have been introduced by the millions of tourists who have poured into Spain and by the many Spaniards who have worked abroad. New ideas have undermined many old traditions. For example, although over 90 per cent of Spaniards are Roman Catholics, less than one out of five regularly attends church. And in 1981, divorce was made legal – a move that would have been impossible ten years earlier.

Above: Religious parades, as here in Zamora, are a reminder of Spain's Roman Catholic traditions.

Below: Barcelona is Spain's second city. Many people have recently moved to the cities.

The land

At the heart of Spain is the Meseta, a huge, dry and largely infertile plateau, with an average height of about 610 m (2,000 ft). Much of the Meseta is flat, though it is crossed by low mountain chains. Most of Spain's major rivers originate in the Meseta. Except for the Guadalquivir, most rivers are unnavigable.

The Meseta is bordered in the north by the Galician and Cantabrian mountains, while the rugged Pyrenees form Spain's border with France in the northeast. Between the Meseta and the Pyrenees is a fertile lowland drained by the Ebro River – the Plains of Aragon. The other main lowlands are in Andalusia.

The Southern Highlands include the Sierra Nevada range, where Mulhacén, the highest peak on the mainland, is situated. The Balearic Islands are an extension of these Highlands in the Mediterranean Sea. The volcanic Canary Islands contain Spain's highest peak, the Pico de Teide on Tenerife, which is 240 m (787 ft) higher than Mulhacén.

Above: The map shows the six land regions in Spain. The central Meseta is the largest.

Below: The southern highlands separate the fertile plains of Andalusia from the southern coast.

In many areas, there is little coastal lowland. However, the coastlands of Asturias in the northwest and Alicante and Valencia in the east are major farming areas.

Northern Spain has a temperate climate, with ample rainfall and lush forests. The Meseta, on the other hand, has a harsh, dry climate, with burning hot summers and bitterly cold winters. The Meseta once had forests and abundant wildlife. But farmers have cut down the trees, turning large areas into scrubland and, in places, semi-desert.

The Mediterranean coast and the Balearic Islands have hot, dry summers and mild, moist winters. The Plains of Andalusia in the south are the hottest part of the Spanish mainland. South of Seville, where the Guadalquivir reaches the sea, is a marshland called Las Marismas. Here, the Coto Donaña National Park is the home of many birds and such threatened animals as the Pardel Lynx.

The Canary Islands have a dry, subtropical climate, with mild and healthy winters.

Above: Much of Spain's northern seacoast on the Atlantic Ocean is lined by cliffs, as here, to the west of Bilbao. Inland lie the Cantabrian Mountains.

Below: The central Meseta is the driest part of Spain. Many arid areas are covered by scrub. Some areas in the south-east are Europe's only deserts.

The people

Casilian Spanish
Galician
Euskara (Basque)
Catalan

The Spaniards are descended from many peoples, including immigrants from Africa and from various parts of Europe. Spain was colonized by the Greeks and Romans, but a Germanic tribe, the Visigoths, seized it in the 5th century AD. In the 8th century, Muslim Moors overran Spain and founded a major civilization there. Christian armies gradually pushed the Moors south, taking Granada, the last Moorish stronghold, in 1492.

These and other elements have been fused to create a people who are varied in appearance and language. The dominant group since the Middle Ages are the Castilians. Castilian Spanish is Spain's official language.

The other main languages are Gallego, Euskara (or Basque) and Catalan. Gallego is spoken in the northwest. The Galicians are a Celtic people. Their famous city of Santiago de Compostela has a cathedral containing the relics of St James the Apostle. It has been a shrine for pilgrims since the Middle Ages.

Above: The main languages and the positions of 16 of the 17 regions of Spain. The 17th region, not on this map, is the Canary Islands. Each region has its own elected government.

Right: On hot summer days, many Spaniards enjoy a cold drink with their friends in open-air restaurants, as here in central Madrid.

Above: Two Basque gardeners take a brief rest.

Below: Roman Catholic nuns are common sights.

Above: A hotel manager in northern Spain.

Below: A motor cycle policeman in Madrid.

The Basques live around the southeast corner of the Bay of Biscay. Their main city is Bilbao. The Basques use a language unrelated to any other in Europe and they may be descendants of western Europe's earliest peoples. The Catalans live in northeast Spain and on the Balearic Islands. Catalan is the first language of five million people. Barcelona is the main Catalan city.

Many people in minority groups have worked for self-government. General Francisco Franco, Spain's dictator from 1939 to 1975, suppressed minority parties. But Spain is now divided into 17 regions, each with its own parliament. Some dissatisfied Basques, however, still support a terrorist group, ETA, which demands full independence.

Spaniards are passionate, courageous, courteous and hospitable people. But their passionate beliefs are sometimes expressed in a violent way. For example, in the fierce Civil War (1936–39), at least 360,000 men, women and children were killed.

Above: A student in Granada.

Below: An architect who works in Granada.

Where people live

Apart from the crowded Madrid region, the central Meseta is thinly populated and the coastal regions contain most of the people. Particularly densely populated are the Basque Region, Catalonia, Valencia and the Canary and Balearic Islands.

In 1986, only 23 per cent of Spaniards lived in country areas, as compared with 75 percent in 1930. The recent rapid drift to cities and tourists resorts where people hope to find jobs and better services for their families has emptied many villages.

Settlements in country areas vary. In the rainy north, the productive land is divided into a patchwork of family-owned smallholdings. Because most farming families live on their own land, the rural population is scattered. But in the dry heartlands of Spain, farms are larger and most people live in villages or small towns. In the south, much of the land is divided into huge estates. Most employees of the great landowners live in large agricultural towns.

Above: Whitewashed houses with shaded verandas are a feature of the countryside.

Below: The Moors built fortresses, such as the Alhambra, in Granada, on easily defended hilltops.

Left: Since the 1960s, many seaside towns and ports, such as Málaga, shown here, have grown quickly to meet the needs of tourists.

Below: Most Spaniards in the cities and towns live in tall apartment buildings. This building is in the Basque Region.

Many great Spanish cities are of ancient origin. Cádiz and Málaga were founded by the Phoenicians, who colonized the coasts in the 9th century BC, while the Carthaginians founded Barcelona in about 230 BC. One Roman city, Córdoba, became capital of Moorish Spain in AD 756. Córdoba, Granada and Seville are examples of cities with superb Arab and Christian buildings.

Modern Spain's largest cities, Madrid and Barcelona, including their suburbs, contain about a fourth of Spain's population. Barcelona is the foremost industrial city and a center of elegance and culture. Other cities with between 500,000 and 1,000,000 people are Valencia, Seville, Zaragoza, and Málaga.

The recent fast growth of cities has created problems. Many unsightly high-rise apartment buildings have been built to provide homes for the expanding populations. Traffic problems are acute, as are problems of pollution. And most recently, urban unemployment and crime rates have increased.

Madrid

Madrid occupies a site where a Moorish fortress was built in the 10th century AD. But it did not become important until 1561, when King Philip II made it the capital of Spain, supposedly because the dry climate was good for his gout. Madrid's climate is the result of the city being so far from the sea and partly because it is about 650 m (2,133 ft) above sea level. Winters are cold, with average temperatures of 5°C (41°F) in January, and summers are hot.

Because of Madrid's central position, it is a focus of communications, as well as Spain's chief administrative and financial center. Since the 1950s, its population has more than doubled, and many industries have sprung up in and around the city. Its products include motor vehicles, chemicals, textiles and leather goods.

Madrid is a lively place, especially when its inhabitants, the *Madrileños*, finish work at 7 p.m. or 8 p.m. The streets fill with people going out for the evening. Restaurants are at their busiest at around 10 p.m. and many people go to the movies at 10.30.

Above: Madrid's Royal Palace is used to entertain visitors. The King's home is the Zarzuela Palace, near Madrid.

Below: A plan of Madrid, showing some of the most famous buildings, streets and other features in this busy and attractive city.

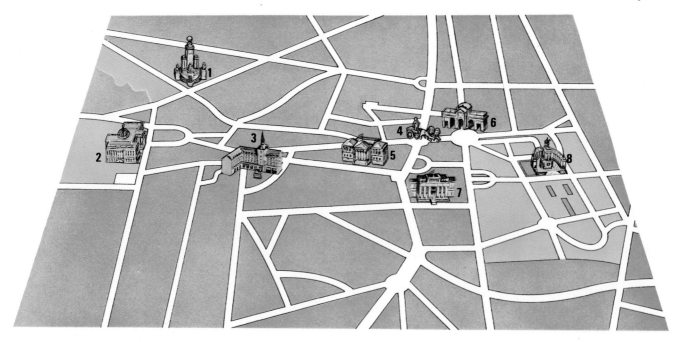

1. Plaza de España
2. Royal Palace
3. Plaza Mayor
4. Plaza des Cibeles
5. Cortes
6. Puerta de Alcala
7. Prado Museum
8. Buen Retiro Park

Left: The monument to the great Spanish writer Miguel de Cervantes stands in Madrid's Plaza de España. In front of the monument are statues of his characters, Don Quixote and Sancho Panza.

Below: Madrid has a good subway system. Most visitors find it the easiest way to travel around the city.

The Prado in Madrid is one of the world's great art galleries, with masterpieces by El Greco, Goya, Velázquez and many others. Another attraction is the Plaza Mayor, a large, 17th-century square where heretics were once burned at the stake. The 18th-century Royal Palace is also open to the public.

Madrid has wide boulevards lined with elegant shops, ornate fountains, a "flea market", the Rastro, quiet parks (notably the Parque del Buen Retiro near the Prado) and many new office towers.

Near Madrid are many places of historic interest. To the south is the beautiful former capital, Toledo. San Lorenzo del Escorial, a monastery and burial place of kings and queens, and the Valley of the Fallen, a Civil War memorial, lie to the north. To the west is Avila, birthplace of St Theresa, Patron Saint of Spain and to the east is Alcalá de Henares, birthplace of the great writer Miguel de Cervantes.

Fact file: land and population

Key Facts

Location: Spain and Portugal share the Iberian peninsula in southwestern Europe. Mainland Spain lies between latitudes 36°N and 43°50'N, and between longitudes 3°15'E and 9°20'W.

Main parts: Spain has 47 mainland provinces and 3 island provinces. The Canary Islands, off the northwest coast of Africa, is divided into two provinces – Las Palmas and Santa Cruz de Tenerife. The third island province consists of the Balearic Islands (notably Mallorca, Minorca and Ibiza) in the Mediterranean Sea. Ceuta and Melilla are two small Spanish enclaves on the north coast of Morocco.

Area: 504,782 sq km (194,897 sq miles).

Population: 39,001,000 (1987 est).

Capital: Madrid.

Major cities:
Madrid (3,188,000)
Barcelona (1,755,000)
Valencia (752,000)
Seville (654,000)
Zaragoza (591,000)
Málaga (503,000)
Bilbao (433,000)
Las Palmas (366,000)
Valladolid (330,000)
Palma de Mallorca (304,000)
Hospitalet (294,000)
Murcia (289,000)

Main languages: Spanish (Castilian) is the official language. Other languages are Basque, Catalan and Galician.

Highest point (*mainland*): Mulhacén in the Sierra Nevada in the southeast, 3,478 m (11,411 ft; (*island*): Pico del Teide on Tenerife in the Canary Islands, 3,718 m (12,198 ft).

Longest river: Tajo (or Tagus), 1,007 km (626 miles) long; it rises in the eastern Meseta and flows west into Portugal where it is called the Tejo. Lisbon stands on its estuary.

°C	°F
19	66
7	45

°C	°F
21	70
9	48

°C	°F
19	67
7	45

°C	°F
19	66
2	36

°C	°F
19	66
4	39

°C	°F
24	76
4	40

°C	°F
23.5	74
8	46

°C	°F
25	77
5	41

°C	°F
24	75
10.6	51

°C	°F
25	77
11	51

°C	°F
24	76
10.6	51

°C	°F
29	84
10.5	51

°C	°F
24	75
13	55

°C	°F
26	79
12	54

°C	°F
24	75
18	64

Average rainfall per year
125-200 cm (50-80")

75-125 cm (30-50")

Less than 75 cm (30")

°C ☐ °F **Average temperature**
January/July

The climate of northern Spain is temperate and rainy. The Meseta has a continental climate, while the south and east coasts have a Mediterranean climate.

USA

AUSTRALIA

FRANCE SPAIN

UK

△ **A land area comparison**
Spain is the second largest country in western Europe after France. It is more than twice as large as the United Kingdom, which covers an area of 244,030 sq km (94,220 sq miles). But Spain is much smaller than the world's largest countries. The USA, with an area of 9,370,000 sq km (3,600,000 sq miles), is more than 18 times bigger than Spain, while Australia, which covers 7,650,000 sq km (2,470,000 sq miles) is more than 15 times as big.

▽ **Spain's cities** and towns have grown quickly in recent years. They now contain more than three out of every four people. Only 50 years ago, three out of four lived in rural areas.

Australia 2 per sq km

USA 25 per sq km

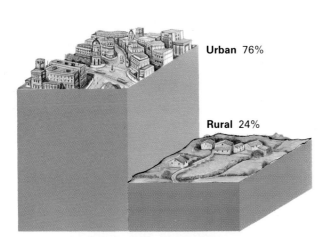

Urban 76%

Rural 24%

Spain 77 per sq km

Britain 231 per sq km

△ **A population density comparison**
By world standards, Spain is fairly thickly populated. But its population density is less than half of the average for Western Europe.

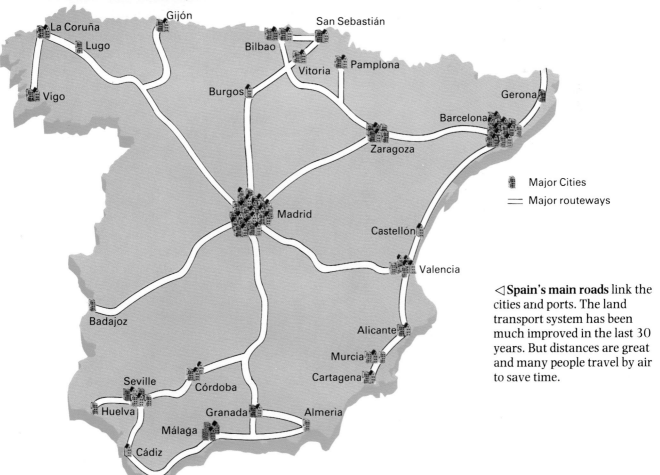

Gijón
La Coruña
Lugo
Vigo
San Sebastián
Bilbao
Vitoria
Pamplona
Burgos
Gerona
Barcelona
Zaragoza

🏙 Major Cities
══ Major routeways

Madrid
Castellón
Valencia
Badajoz
Alicante
Murcia
Cartagena
Seville
Córdoba
Huelva
Granada
Almeria
Málaga
Cádiz

◁ **Spain's main roads** link the cities and ports. The land transport system has been much improved in the last 30 years. But distances are great and many people travel by air to save time.

Home life

The family is the most important institution in Spanish society and the mother represents the center of the family. When someone is ill or becomes unemployed, members of the family help out. In the 1980s, more than nine out of every ten young people lived with their parents or with another relation, a higher proportion than in most of western Europe.

While most country families live in whitewashed clay or stone houses, most city people live in apartments, usually in tall buildings. Nearly seven-tenths of families have bought or are buying their homes. Living standards have risen in recent years.

Increased comfort is not the only recent change in home life. Under the rule of General Francisco Franco, women had to get a certificate proving their husbands' approval before they could take a job. But today more and more married women have jobs. Girls and single women were once kept under strict family control until they married, but young people now mix freely.

Above: Señor Francisco and Señora Filito Ballesteros look down from the balcony of their modern apartment in Granada.

Right: Most people in Spain spend a lot of time watching television.

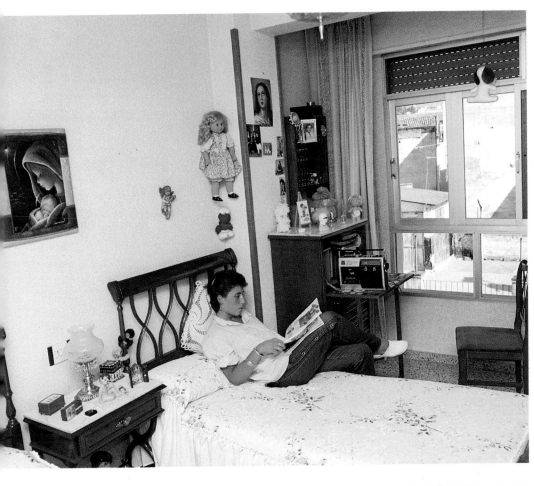

Left: Paz Ballesteros has her own room, where she can listen to the radio or to records without being interrupted.

Below: The family enjoys an afternoon cup of coffee in the dining room.

In the past, visitors were amazed to find that everything happened much later in the day in Spain than elsewhere. This was because workers and children went home between 1 and 4 p.m. for a leisurely lunch and a *siesta*, or afternoon nap. People then worked late and did not have their evening meal until 10 or 11 p.m. The entire family, including the children, did not go to sleep until midnight or later.

This pattern of home life, which is well suited to warm countries, is now under attack. The government and some employers would like people to work a continuous 8-hour day, although a majority of people still want their long afternoon break. Another old tradition, the evening *paseo*, when the entire family takes a walk before dinner, is also being replaced – by television viewing. Not all old customs are on the way out, especially in country areas. For example a long courtship period, called a *noviazgo*, which is closely supervised, still precedes most weddings.

Shops and shopping

Shopping hours follow the same timetable as working hours – that is, shops close between about 1 and 4 p.m., but stay open in the evening until 8 p.m. or even later. Food shops open on Sunday, but everything closes on national holidays and for local fiestas.

Because it is so warm, most Spanish families eat more fish, fruit and fresh vegetables than people in cooler European countries. In the past, shoppers have bought fresh produce either from small local shops or, in the cities, from large, glass-covered markets, which contain row upon row of stalls. These markets offer a wide range of food at lower prices than local shops. Small shops and markets still exist but supermarkets are gaining ground, especially in the cities and tourist resorts. People find supermarkets more convenient and cleaner than most other shops. For clothes, household goods and many other items, Spain has several chains of excellent department stores, including Galerías Preciados, El Corte Inglés and Woolworths.

Above: Street markets, together with large covered markets in the cities, are places where fresh food is cheap.

Below: Many Spaniards still prefer to shop at small, family-run shops, which have a friendly atmosphere.

Left: Supermarkets attract many shoppers as elsewhere in Europe. They are convenient and offer a wide range of products.

Above: A selection of sausages and cheese.

Below: Some of the items from a shopping bag.

Most Spaniards are dress-conscious and their clothes, including leather jackets, suede coats, kidskin gloves, shoes and boots, are of high quality. Many visitors to Spain buy these products.

Each region and many cities and towns have their own special products. Catalonia is famed for its textiles, Alicante and the Balearic Islands for their shoes, Granada and Murcia for their rugs and carpets, Manises, near Valencia, for beautiful ceramics, and Toledo for its damascene ware (inlaid metalware), including highly decorated knives and swords.

Handicrafts which are exported on a large scale include castanets, dolls and other toys, embroideries, fans, glassware, lace and wineskins. Some of the best places to buy handicrafts are the government-run handicraft stores, called *Artespana*. Prices in these stores are fixed, as in most department stores and shops. But bargaining is permissible in the flea markets and in some antique shops.

Cooking and eating

Spain is a large country and has many famous regional dishes. Northern Spain is known for its sauces and fish dishes, including cod and hake from the Atlantic Ocean. One well-known dish in Asturias is *fabada*, a stew made with beans, sausage and other meats. Central Spain is known for its roasts, but stews are popular on chilly winter days. For example, *Cocido a la Madrileña* consists of stewing steak, bones and ham boiled in water with vegetables.

Eastern Spain is famed for its rice dishes. The best known is *paella*, which is named after the shallow iron pan in which the rice, seafood and other items are cooked. Southern Spain is known for fish dishes cooked in olive oil. *Gazpacho*, a cold soup made from vegetables liquefied in a blender, originated in Andalusia.

Wine is drunk with most meals. A popular drink on hot days is *sangría*, a mixture of wine, soda water, ice and fruit. Soft drinks include *horchata*, made from tiger-nuts. Coffee, usually served black, is the most popular hot drink.

Above: Filita Ballesteros prepares a meal for her family.

Left: Paella is perhaps Spain's best known dish. It contains rice, seafood, meat, red peppers and other items.

Left: Meals being prepared in the kitchen of a family restaurant in Granada.

Below: Lunch in Spain consists of several courses. In this restaurant, the first course is an omelette, followed by fish. Wine is drunk with the meal.

Breakfast (*desayuno*) normally consists of coffee or hot chocolate, with croissants, toast or *churros* (strips of dough). Mid-morning snacks include toasted sandwiches or a *bocadillo* (a roll containing ham, squid or even a cold omelette).

Around 1 p.m., when the lunch break begins, many people have an aperitif in a bar and sample the *tapas* (snacks) on the counter. These include plates of artichokes, cheese, olives, shrimps and spicy sausage. Lunch (*almuerzo*) is for many the main meal of the day, consisting of three or four courses with wine. The first course may be soup or an egg dish, such as an omelette with potatoes, followed by fish, a meat dish and a dessert.

When children get home from school, they have a light meal (*merienda*), which usually includes pastries and cakes. Later comes the evening meal (*cena*). Reasonably affluent families may have two evening meals a week in restaurants, where they have a three or four course meal. When they eat at home, they often prefer a lighter, cold meal.

Pastimes and sports

After a day's work, many Spaniards enjoy meeting their friends in village squares or open-air cafes. At weekends, family picnics are popular and today, as incomes have increased, many families spend their annual vacations by the sea. Many teenagers, enjoy rock music and dancing in discotheques.

Central to Spanish life are *fiestas*, or popular festivals. Some, such as the celebrations in Holy Week, are national. Others are held to celebrate a local saint. People wear traditional dress and organize music, dances and often a bullfight.

Most cities in Spain have at least one bullring. In 1985, a total of 31.6 million spectators attended bullfights. But a recent survey showed that 50 per cent of Spaniards were not interested in or were opposed to bullfighting. The financial success of this spectacle now depends to a large extent on the attendance of foreign tourists.

One distinctive Spanish sport is *pelota vasca* or *jai alai*. This fast ball game played in a walled concrete court originated in the Basque Region.

Above: On hot days, people relax in the shade in town or village squares.

Below left: Bullfights are held in all the main cities.

Below: Pelota is a fast ball game played in the Basque Region. The ball is hurled against a wall with the bare hand or with basketwork rackets.

Left: Soccer is Spain's most popular spectator sport. Here, excited fans wave flags at an international match in Madrid.

Below: One of Spain's best known international sportspersons is the brilliant golfer, Severiano Ballesteros.

The leading spectator sport is soccer. The season runs from September to May and first class matches are usually played on Sundays. Some clubs, such as Real Madrid and Barcelona, are famous far beyond the borders of Spain. Under the rule of General Francisco Franco, when regional politics were banned, soccer clubs became symbols of a region's identity. For example, the Basques regarded a win for Atletico Bilbao as a victory for Basque nationalism.

Golf has become increasingly popular. It is played throughout the year. Spain now has more than 80 golf courses, most of which are around the coasts. Water sports, including sea fishing, sailing, swimming, water skiing and wind surfing, are also extremely popular. The greatest number of winter resorts are in the Pyrenees, but winter sports centres are also found in the Cantabrian Mountains, the Guadarrama range near Madrid, and the Sierra Nevada, near Granada.

News and broadcasting

Spaniards are not great newspaper readers and only about one person out of every five regularly reads a newspaper. There are no truly national daily papers, though a few, including *ABC*, *Ya* and *El País*, can be bought outside the area in which they were originally published.

From 1939 to 1975, newspapers were censored. As a result, they were dull and often did not report important events. But freedom of the press is now guaranteed by the 1978 Constitution and newspapers are helping to shape public opinion, although their impact is not as great as that of the radio or television. *El País*, which was founded in 1976, has the highest circulation. Since 1983, it has been published in both Barcelona and Madrid.

About two out of every five Spaniards rely on the radio for news. The government network, *Radio Nacional de España*, can be heard throughout Spain and it broadcasts in all the national languages. There are also many private and religious stations. One private network, the *Radio Cadena Española*, claims a quarter of all radio listeners.

Above: A stand in Madrid which sells newspapers, magazines and books.

Left: A selection of women's magazines and children's comic books.

Left: The front pages of Spain's best selling newspapers.

Below: *Hola* is a magazine which gives news about rich and famous people.

Above: The cover of the weekly magazine which lists television and radio programs.

Below: Julio Iglesias is one of Spain's internationally known popular singers.

Television is extremely popular in Spain. Introduced in 1956, it was highly censored until 1975. Today, the government-run *Radiotelevisión Española* (RTVE) transmits two channels. There are also two private stations – one broadcasting in Catalan (*TV3*) and the other in Basque (*TV Vasca*).

Of the two main channels, one concentrates on popular programs and shows the majority of the advertisements. The second channel includes some "quality" programs, News and news-related programs, old films, especially North American ones, and sport take up the bulk of the time. Foreign soap operas dubbed into Spanish also have huge followings. About 70 per cent of Spaniards form their political opinions from television viewing. The RTVE has been accused of pro-government propaganda, and the government has announced long-term plans to create three independent commercial stations.

Fact File: home life and leisure

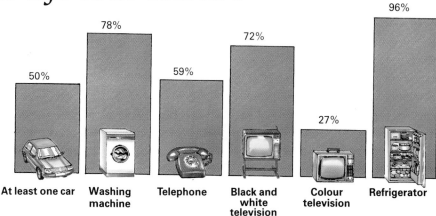

At least one car	Washing machine	Telephone	Black and white television	Colour television	Refrigerator
50%	78%	59%	72%	27%	96%

Key Facts

Population composition: In 1985, people under 15 years of age made up 24.6 percent of the population; people between 15 and 60 made up 59.5 percent; and people over 60 years of age made up 15.9 percent. Women formed 50.8 percent of the population.

Average life expectancy at birth: 76 years in 1986, as compared with 72 years in 1970.

Rate of population increase: 0.5 percent per year (1980–87), as compared with 0.4 per cent in Europe as a whole (excluding the USSR).

Family life: The marriage rate in 1984 was 0.5 per 1,000 people. The average size of households was 2.8 persons. Most people have at least one full month's vacation per year. Most Spaniards holiday in Spain.

Work: A 40 hour week was agreed between employer's organizations and trade unions in 1983. the minimum monthly wage in January 1988 was 44,040 pesetas (roughly US $388, or £218). The workforce in 1987 was 13.894.000, while the unemployed represented nearly 22 percent of the workforce, the highest rate in Europe.

Prices: In 1965–80, the average yearly inflation rate was 11.8 percent. In 1980–86, it was 11.3 percent.

Religion: There is no official religion, but most Spaniards belong to the Roman Church. (In 1981, an estimated 82.7 percent of all children born were baptized into the Roman Catholic Church.) There are also about 150,000 other Christians and 13,000 Jews.

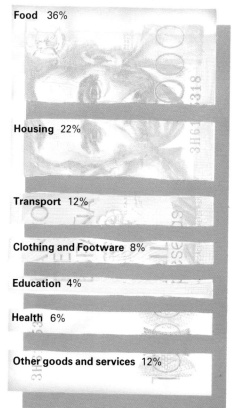

Food 36%

Housing 22%

Transport 12%

Clothing and Footware 8%

Education 4%

Health 6%

Other goods and services 12%

△ **The percentage of households owning various items**
Almost all Spanish households own a television set and a refrigerator, which is extremely useful in the hot summer. The percentage of households with a car is lower than the average for the EEC.

◁ **How the average household budget is spent**
The percentage of income spent on food has been falling as real incomes have increased.

▽ **Spanish currency and stamps**
The unit of Spanish currency is the peseta, which is divided up into 100 céntimos. Since July 1984, however, céntimos have not been in legal use. In 1988, there were about 200 pesetas to the British pound and 113 to the US dollar.

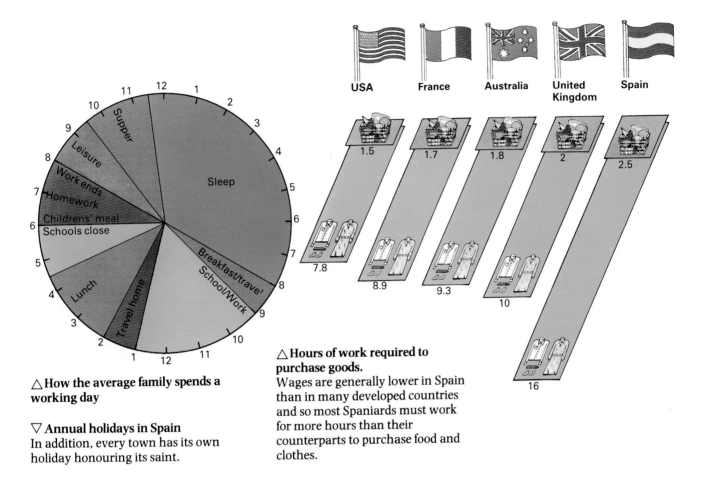

△ **How the average family spends a working day**

▽ **Annual holidays in Spain**
In addition, every town has its own holiday honouring its saint.

△ **Hours of work required to purchase goods.**
Wages are generally lower in Spain than in many developed countries and so most Spaniards must work for more hours than their counterparts to purchase food and clothes.

USA | France | Australia | United Kingdom | Spain

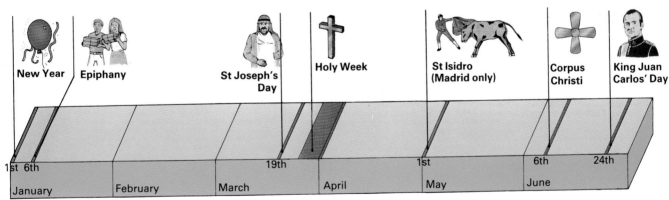

New Year — Epiphany — St Joseph's Day — Holy Week — St Isidro (Madrid only) — Corpus Christi — King Juan Carlos' Day

1st 6th — 19th — 1st — 6th 24th

January | February | March | April | May | June

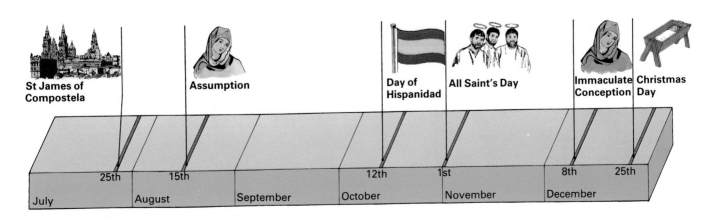

St James of Compostela — Assumption — Day of Hispanidad — All Saint's Day — Immaculate Conception — Christmas Day

25th — 15th — 12th — 1st — 8th 25th

July | August | September | October | November | December

Farming and fishing

In the mid–1980s, farming, forestry and fishing employed about 16 out of every 100 people, as compared with 26 in 1970. This change reflects the shift of people from the country to the cities.

Spain is one of Europe's top agricultural countries, although much of the land is dry and must be irrigated to make it productive. Cereals occupy the largest area of cropland. The two leading cereals are barley and wheat. Spain is the world's top producer of olive oil and is among the world's top five producers of citrus fruits and wine. The best-known wine-producing region is probably that around Jerez, where the fortified wine called sherry is made. Other famous wines come from La Rioja, a region in the north. Spain produces many other fruits besides citrus fruits and grapes. They include apples and pears in the northwest and almonds, apricots, figs and peaches in the sunny east and southeast.

Sheep are important on the Meseta and wool is a major product. Cattle rearing is also important, especially dairy cattle in the wet north. Goats are kept in the dry southeast.

Above: Goats are reared in parts of the Meseta. Goats are greedy animals. They lay the land bare and so they cause soil erosion.

Below: Many large farms in Spain are mechanized. Here, wheat is being harvested in northern Spain.

Above: These large olive groves are in Andalusia in southern Spain. Spain is the world's leading producer of olive oil.

Right: Valencia is famed for its lemons and other citrus fruits.
Below right: Fishing is important in the north.

Many forests have been cut down and, together with overgrazing, this has exposed large areas to the wind and rain. Soil erosion has made some of these areas infertile. Another problem is that long droughts sometimes occur, as in the early 1980s. They reduce crop production and many farm animals die.

Most of Spain's forests are in the wet north, although plantations of trees are now being planted in dry areas to counter soil erosion. One important tree is the cork oak whose bark is used to make corks for wine bottles.

Fishing is a major industry and Spain has one of the world's largest fishing fleets. The main fishing ports are in the north and northwest, where the people fish in the Atlantic Ocean. There is also a fishing industry in the Mediterranean Sea. Important catches include anchovies, cod, hake, sardines and tuna. Molluscs and crustaceans are also caught.

Resources and industry

Spain has many mineral deposits, though some have been overworked and are now expensive to mine. However, Spain does not have enough minerals for its present needs and must import most of them.

The most important resources are found in the north, including high-grade iron ore in the Cantabrian Mountains and brown coal (lignite) and anthracite in the Asturias region, south of Oviedo. These materials have long been used to manufacture iron and steel. Spain's other minerals include copper, lead, manganese, mercury, potash, tungsten, uranium and zinc.

About three-tenths of Spain's electricity is produced at hydroelectric power stations. But although Spain is mountainous, the lack of rain has restricted the development of water power. In 1987, Spain produced about 1.6 million tons of petroleum. This is far less than the country needs and most of the oil is imported. This makes Spain vulnerable to rises in world oil prices. Such rises cause economic problems.

Above: Hydroelectric power stations have been built in mountainous areas, such as in the foothills of the Pyrenees.

Below: Cement is produced at this open-cast quarry west of Barcelona. Spain has recently become a major industrial country.

Left: Spain exports more cars than any other West European country. The car industry is dominated by foreign companies, such as the Ford Motor Company.

Below: The manufacture of silicon chips and microprocessors is growing quickly in Spain. Such new technology will give Spain an industrial advantage in the years to come.

Many old industries, such as the manufacture of tiles which began under the Moors, still survive in Spain. Wool and cotton textiles are leading manufactures, as also are clothes, chemicals and fertilizers, footwear and processed foods.

Since the 1950s, however, Spain has undergone a second Industrial Revolution. Industries that have grown quickly include vehicle manufacture, machine tools, steel, textiles, domestic appliances and shipbuilding, although the latter has been hit recently by the world recession. Spain is one of the world's top car makers and western Europe's biggest exporter. By 1984, the car industry was Spain's biggest single industrial employer.

The most recent developments are in the field of electronics, information technology and industrial design. In the mid-1980s, work began, outside Madrid, on western Europe's largest microchip factory. It was financed by the Spanish Telephone Company and the American Telephone and Telegraph Company.

Tourism

Only 50 years ago, only rich Europeans went abroad for their vacations. After World War II, however, as family incomes rose, a new tourist industry developed, offering low-cost vacations on the sunny Mediterranean coasts of Italy and Spain. From 1950, when tourism was almost non-existent, many coastal resorts were developed. In 1959, about 4 million tourists visited Spain. In 1986, the number of tourists per year reached 47 million.
million.
providing jobs for poor farmers and fishermen. The Spanish government set up training courses for tourism-related jobs, such as hotel managers, guides and cooks. It fixed prices, prevented overcharging and constantly checked to see that tourists got good value for their money. The money spent by tourists enabled Spain to pay for much-needed imports and to develop services, such as health care, which benefit everyone. Today, tourism employs about a tenth of all Spanish workers.

Above: Benidorm is a highly developed seaside resort on the Costa Blanca, northeast of Alicante.

Left: The Cathedral in Santiago de Compostela in Galicia contains what are thought to be the remains of the Apostle St James. It attracts pilgrims and tourists.

Left: Spain has many fascinating old towns, such as Avila, west of Madrid, which was the birthplace of St Theresa. The old town is surrounded by superb medieval walls.

Below: Some resorts, such as here on Tenerife in the Canary Islands, have lost their Spanish character and gained an international one. Tourism has changed many areas and destroyed some former beauty spots.

In the early 1980s, the greatest numbers of tourists came from France, Portugal, Britain and West Germany. The single most popular resort area was Mallorca in the Balearic Islands. On the mainland, most people still headed for the Mediterranean coasts.

Inland Spain also has much to offer, including fascinating medieval towns and castles, Moorish palaces, magnificent churches and great art galleries. There are many fine hotels, including Paradores (National Tourist Inns), many of which are ancient monuments converted into modern hotels. A more neglected area is the scenic north.

Tourism has contributed to social change. The visitors have introduced new ideas, such as the free mingling of young men and women. Many young Spaniards wanted, and were soon given this same freedom. The growth of tourist resorts has also destroyed many beauty spots and it has caused pollution. Fortunately an increasing number of Spaniards are now aware of the urgent need for conservation.

Transportation

In the early 1930s, Spain had one of Western Europe's poorest transport systems. During the Civil War in the late 1930s, roads, railways and shipping all suffered great damage.

In the last 30 years, however, great changes have occurred. Spain's highways are among the busiest in Europe, especially around the coasts. Some have toll gates where motorists pay to use the motorway. Spain now employs a large force of traffic police. One out of every two Spanish families owns a car, but many people still use buses both in the cities and in the countryside. Madrid and Barcelona also have *metros* (subway systems).

Spanish National Railways (RENFE) have electrified nearly half of the rail network, while the equipment, locomotives and many stations have been modernized. Fares depend on the type of train. Ordinary trains, called *expresos* or *rápidos*, are the cheapest. Fast trains, including the TER and ELT (*electrotrén*), are more expensive, while the most costly are the luxury TALGO trains.

Above: This highway cuts across pleasant countryside to the east of Bilbao. Trucks now carry the bulk of Spain's internal trade.

Below: Spain has excellent fast trains. But some visitors find it hard to understand the complicated fare structure on the various kinds of trains.

Air travel is important, because distances are great and road and rail travel can sometimes be too slow for people with limited time. Air travel is also the quickest way to get to the Balearic and Canary islands. Two national airlines, Iberia and Avaco, operate domestic flights, while Iberia is also a major international airline. Madrid, Palma de Mallorca and Barcelona have the three airports with the greatest passenger traffic.

Excluding fishing vessels, the Spanish merchant fleet ranked 17th in the world in total tonnage in 1986. It handles much of Spain's foreign trade and some internal trade, but the bulk of domestic freights is carried by road. There are also important cargo lines linking Spain to North and South America. The largest ports are Barcelona and Bilbao. Other major ports are Algeciras, Cartagena, La Coruña, Gijón, Huelva, Las Palmas and Santa Cruz de Tenerife in the Canary Islands, Málaga and Valencia.

Above: Iberia operates regular services to Europe, the Americas, Africa and the Middle East.

Below: Bilbao is a major port and manufacturing city. It has a huge iron and steel industry.

Fact file: economy and trade

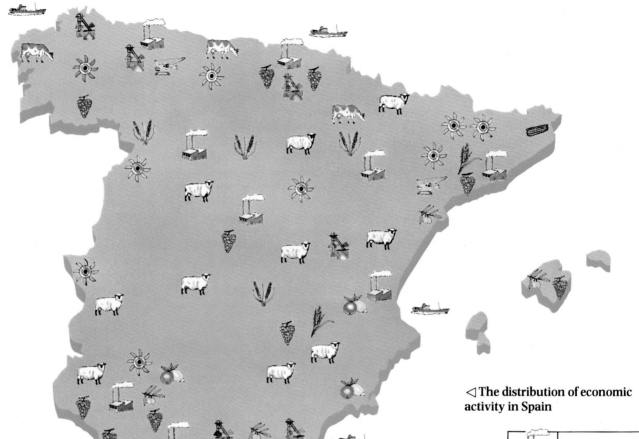

◁ **The distribution of economic activity in Spain**

	Industry
	Iron ore mining
	Hydroelectric plant
	Coal and lignite
	Sheep
	Cattle
	Wheat
	Barley
	Grapes
	Citrus fruit
	Cork
	Olives
	Fishing

Key Facts

Structure of production: Of the total gross domestic product (the GDP, or the value of all economic activity in Spain), farming, forestry and fishing contribute 6 per cent, industry 37 per cent, and services 57 per cent.

Farming and forestry: Most of the land is used for growing crops, for grazing, or for forestry, but production is generally low and Spain must import food. *Main products:* barley, citrus fruits, cork, grapes (for wine-making), corn, oats, rye, wheat, wool.

Livestock: cattle, 5.8 million; sheep, 17.1 million; pigs, 15.8 million; poultry, 53 million.

Fishing: The catch (1986), including anchovy, hake, sardines and whiting, was 1.05 million tonnes.

Mining: Spain's leading mineral resource is high-grade iron ore. Spain produces some coal and lignite (brown coal). Other minerals include copper, lead, mercury, zinc.

Energy: Of the total electricity output (1986), generators powered by coal, oil or gas produced 50 per cent, hydroelectric stations 21 per cent, and nuclear power plants 29 per cent.

Manufacturing: Major industries include the manufacture of textiles, cement, steel, chemicals and oil products. The largest single employer is the car industry.

Trade: (1986): *Total imports:* US $34,920 million; *exports:* $27,132 million. Spain is the world's 14th most important trading nation.

Economic growth: The average real growth rate of Spain's gross national product (GNP) between 1980 and 1987 was 1.6 per cent per year.

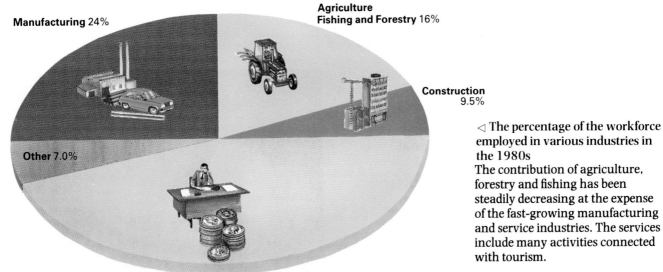

Manufacturing 24%

Agriculture Fishing and Forestry 16%

Construction 9.5%

Other 7.0%

Trades, public and personal services 43.5%

◁ The percentage of the workforce employed in various industries in the 1980s
The contribution of agriculture, forestry and fishing has been steadily decreasing at the expense of the fast-growing manufacturing and service industries. The services include many activities connected with tourism.

▷ **Spain's main trading partners in the 1980s**
In 1986, the year in which Spain became a member of the EEC, 54.7 per cent of its trade was with the other 11 EEC countries.

Spanish Exports

Spanish Imports

2.1 1.9
UK

2.3 1.5
Rest of EEC

2.3 3.2
West Germany

2.4 3.2
USA

3.7 2.8
France

0.7 0.7
Eastern Europe

1.7 1.4
Italy

1.4 3.4
Latin America

6.1 8.9

1.4 2.8
Middle East

Rest of World

▽ **The types of items imported and exported by Spain in the 1980s**
Spain lacks oil and so it has to import large quantities of this fuel. As a result, when world oil prices rise, Spain suffers many economic problems.

3.3 **Food and Drink** 3.7

1.4 **Raw materials** 1.1

10.6 **Oil products** 2.2

12.7 **Manufactures** 15.3

1.8 **Others** 1.8

(in thousand million US dollars)

Education

In 1900, about 60 out of every 100 Spaniards could not read or write. By 1987, only 3 per cent of people over 14 were illiterate and most Spanish parents now encourage their children to go as far as possible in the educational system.

The first stage of education is at a private nursery school, but attendance is not compulsory. Compulsory primary, or basic, education begins at the age of 6 and continues until 13. At 14, many students begin a three-year *bachillerato* course, at the end of which successful students obtain the title *bachiller*. Students with this title then spend one more year taking a course which prepares them for university. Students are given vocational training.

Primary education is free at government schools. But about a third of pupils attend private primary and secondary schools, many of which are run by the Church. Some government grants and scholarships are available for students at private schools.

Above: Two Spanish schoolchildren relax.
Below left: A typical Spanish classroom.

Below: All Spanish children start their secondary education, at the age of 14.

Left: Computers are now common educational tools in most Spanish schools. Most students also find them fun to use.

Below: Opportunities for secondary and higher education have increased in recent years, because Spain needs highly qualified young people.

Educational opportunities have increased rapidly in recent years. The most striking changes have occurred in secondary and higher education. For example, only one out of every 20 workers in 1964 had attended secondary schools or technical centers. By 1980, 24 per cent of the nation had received education beyond the primary level.

Between 1977 and 1985, enrollment in secondary schools and vocational colleges, universities and other institutions increased by nearly a third, while the number of people between 20 and 29 taking educational courses increased by nearly 50 per cent. This includes training people for new industries.

In 1986, Spain had 33 universities in all. This figure includes a National University for Education at Home, which operates by mail from Madrid, using radio and television for teaching purposes. However, problems remain, such as maintaining the standards required by university graduates in the rest of Europe.

The arts

Spain has long artistic traditions in architecture, painting, literature and music. In the 8th century Spain was invaded by the Moors. They were great architects who built beautiful mosques and *alcazares* (fortified palaces), such as the Alhambra, in Granada. Spain also has many fine medieval churches. One of the most famous Christian buildings is the unfinished Church of the Sagrada Familia, in Barcelona. It is the work of the Catalan architect, Antonio Gaudí (1852–1926).

Painters include El Greco (1541–1614), who was born in Crete, though he did most of his work in Spain; the great court painter Diego Velázquez (1599–1660); and Francisco Goya (1746–1828), some of whose paintings depict the horrors of war. Probably the best known 20th-century painter is the Spaniard Pablo Picasso (1881–1973), who pioneered the Cubist style. Another famous painter is the surrealist, Salvador Dali (1904–89).

Above: The Moors left many superb examples of their Islamic art in Spain. Perhaps their greatest work is the Alhambra in Granada.

Left: The Church of the Sagrada Familia, Barcelona, is the unfinished masterpiece of the Catalan architect Antonio Gaudí.

Left: Diego Velázquez painted this portrait of Prince Balthasar Carlos.

Below: The greater painter, Pablo Picasso, did most of his work in France.

Above: Don Quixote and his servant Sancho Panza, creations of Miguel de Cervantes, are the two best known characters in the whole of Spanish literature.

The Golden Age of Spanish literature, from the mid-16th to the late 17th centuries, produced the great writer Miguel de Cervantes (1547–1616). His *Don Quixote* tells of a landowner who imagines he is a knight fighting injustice. Although a comic novel, it also treats serious issues of universal concern. Other writers of this period are two dramatists, Lope de Vega (1562–1635) and Pedro Calderón de la Barca (1600–81). In recent times, two essayists, Miguel de Unamuno (1864–1936) and José Ortega y Gasset (1883–1955), won worldwide fame, as also did the poet and playwright, Federico García Lorca (1898–1936).

Spain has produced fine guitar music and lively dances, such as flamenco. The best known recent composer, Manuel de Falla (1876–1946), wrote the exciting ballet *The Three-Cornered Hat*.

Spain's best known film director Luis Buñuel (1900–80) worked mostly in exile because he opposed General Franco. His first movies were made in Paris with Salvador Dali.

The making of modern Spain

Two events of great importance to Spain occurred in 1492. First, Spanish forces finally ended Moorish rule in southern Spain. Second, Spain sent Christopher Columbus, a Genoese navigator, on a voyage of discovery. He sailed to the West Indies and discovered a New World.

Following Columbus came Spanish soldiers and settlers. By 1550, Spain ruled part of what is now the southwestern USA, Mexico, Central America, most of the West Indies and most of western South America.

In the late 16th century, a series of wars with England, France and the Netherlands began to weaken Spain. Particularly serious was the loss of half of the Armada (Spanish fleet) in 1588. Spain gradually declined. In 1808, France invaded Spain. Although the French were driven out in 1813, Spain's control of its empire had been weakened. By 1825, Spain had lost all its empire except Cuba, Puerto Rico, the Philippines, Guam and some African territories. After a war with the USA in 1898, the only colonies left were those in Africa.

Above: A Mexican painting of Hernán Cortés in action. Cortés conquered Mexico and Spain won a huge empire.

Below: The defeat of the Spanish Armada in 1588 began the decline of Spain as a major world power.

Left: Spain lost Cuba after her defeat by the United States in 1898.

Above: The Spanish Civil War divided families and was bitterly fought.

Below: General Franco ruled Spain until 1975. He was a dictator opposed to change, but during his rule, Spain became increasingly open to outside influences.

In the early 20th century, Spain was one of Europe's poorest countries. Agriculture was the main industry.

Spain was also politically divided. In 1931, elections held in the cities returned a large majority of republicans to power and so King Alfonso XIII left the country. After a general election, a government was formed by republicans, liberals, socialists and others.

But unrest continued. Monarchists opposed republicans; Catalans demanded self-government; and poverty increased because of the world economic depression. In 1936, an alliance of republicans, socialists and communists, called the Popular Front, won a general election. The army rose in revolt and made General Francisco Franco its leader. The Spanish Civil War continued until 1939, when Franco became Chief of State. Franco ruled Spain as a dictator until his death in 1975. He restored peace and stability, but he did so at the expense of the liberty of the individual.

Spain in the modern world

In 1969, General Franco nominated as his successor Prince Juan Carlos de Borbón, the grandson of Alfonso XIII who had been born in exile in 1938. When Franco died, the Prince became King Juan Carlos I, and he quickly used his considerable power to restore democracy.

In 1978, a Constitution agreed by popular vote made Spain a parliamentary democracy. The King was Head of State, but did not have any direct role in government. The right of Spain's 17 Regions to run their own local affairs was also guaranteed. In 1980, the Basques and Catalans elected their own regional parliaments, followed by the Galicians in 1981 and the Andalusians in 1982.

Some members of the armed forces thought that the changes went too far. In 1981, an uprising failed largely because the King persuaded other military leaders to stay loyal. Other groups, such as the Basque terrorist organization ETA, thought that the changes were insufficient.

Below left: An attempt by army officers to overthrow the government in 1981.
Below: Basque ETA spokesmen at a press conference.

Above: King Juan Carlos I and Queen Sophia were greeted by the Prince and Princess of Wales on their arrival in Britain on an official visit in 1986.

In 1982, the Spanish Workers Socialist Party PSOE) won the general election. Its leader, Felipe González, became prime minister. To expand Spain's trading opportunities, he negotiated Spain's entry into the European Economic Community (EEC) in 1986. EEC membership has also brought increased competition. Older industries are declining and being replaced by more efficient ones. Such changes, together with the general world recession, have caused problems. In 1986, 20 per cent of Spain's workforce was unemployed.

Spain also faces a dispute over the British colony of Gibraltar on the southern tip of the Iberian peninsula. Spain claims Gibraltar, but Britain says that no change will occur unless the 30,000 Gibraltarians agree to it.

The return to democracy has not revived the political divisions of the 1930s. Instead, the chance of a better life has weakened support for extremist groups. Modern Spanish society is remarkably stable and most people, especially the young, regard the future with confidence.

Above left: A political rally in Las Palmas in 1986.
Above: Felipe González was elected prime minister in 1982 and in 1986.

Below: Young Spaniards now have the freedom to choose their own lifestyles, a freedom which was largely denied to their parents.

Fact File: government and world role

Key Facts

Official name: *España.*

Flag: Three horizontal stripes of red, yellow and red.

National anthem: *Marcha real* (Royal march).

National government: Spain is a parliamentary monarchy. *Head of State:* the monarch, Juan Carlos I (born 1938), who became King in 1975 following the death of Spain's dictator, Francisco Franco. *Legislature:* the Cortes (parliament) consists of two elected houses – the Congress of Deputies, which has not less than 300 and not more than 400 members, and the Senate, with 208 members who represent the provinces. *Executive:* the President of the Government (or prime minister) and the Council of Ministers (cabinet). The prime minister, the leader of the majority party in the Cortes, is elected by the Congress of Deputies.

Armed forces: A period of military service is compulsory for men between 21 and 35. *Army:* 230,000 personnel in 1988; *Navy:* 64,700 personnel in 1988; *Air force:* 32,500 personnel and 215 combat aircraft in 1988.

Economic alliances: Since January 1, 1986, Spain has been a member of the European Economic Community (or Common Market). It also belongs to the OECD (Organization for Economic Co-operation and Development).

Political alliances: Spain is a member of the United Nations, the Council of Europe and, since May 1982, of the western defense alliance, NATO (North Atlantic Treaty Organization).

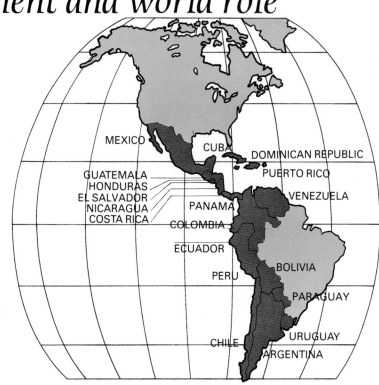

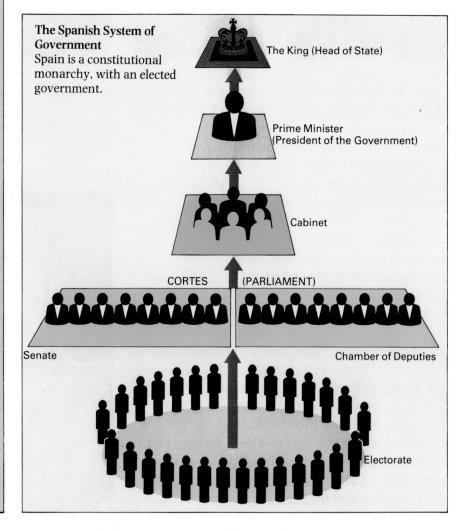

The Spanish System of Government
Spain is a constitutional monarchy, with an elected government.

The King (Head of State)

Prime Minister (President of the Government)

Cabinet

CORTES (PARLIAMENT)

Senate

Chamber of Deputies

Electorate

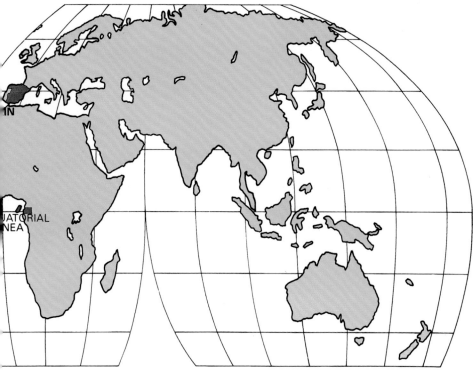

◁ **Where the Spanish language is spoken**
Spanish is used for official purposes in many countries besides Spain. It is the chief language in Central and South America.

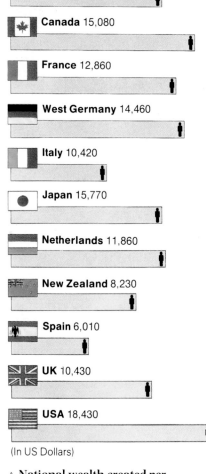

Australia 10,900

Belgium 11,360

Canada 15,080

France 12,860

West Germany 14,460

Italy 10,420

Japan 15,770

Netherlands 11,860

New Zealand 8,230

Spain 6,010

UK 10,430

USA 18,430

(In US Dollars)

▽ **The European Economic Community**
The EEC has now grown from six to twelve members. Spain and Portugal joined the EEC in 1986. They hope to benefit before long from belonging to what is now the world's largest trading community.

△ **National wealth created per person in 1987**
Spain's annual production rose rapidly from the 1960s. However, in terms of its wealth per person Spain ranks ninth in the EEC with a per capita GNP which is about the same as that of Ireland. Only Greece and Portugal have lower figures.

Index